Smart Fast Food Meals

HOW TO EAT HEALTHY AT THE TOP 12 RESTAURANTS

Peggy Reinhardt, MPH, LN

John Wiley & Sons, Inc.
New York • Chichester • Weinheim • Brisbane • Singapore • Toronto

This book is printed on acid-free paper. ∞

Copyright © 1999 by Peggy Reinhardt, MPH, LN
All rights reserved

Published by John Wiley & Sons, Inc.

Published simultaneously in Canada

No part of this publication may be reproduced, stored in a retrieval system or transmitted in any form or by any means, electronic, mechanical, photocopying, recording, scanning or otherwise, except as permitted under Sections 107 or 108 of the 1976 United States Copyright Act, without either the prior written permission of the Publisher, or authorization through payment of the appropriate per-copy fee to the Copyright Clearance Center, 222 Rosewood Drive, Danvers, MA 01923, (978) 750-8400, fax (978) 750-4744. Requests to the Publisher for permission should be addressed to the Permissions Department, John Wiley & Sons, Inc., 605 Third Avenue, New York, NY 10158-0012, (212) 850-6011, fax (212) 850-6008, E-Mail: PERMREQ @ WILEY.COM.

The information contained in this book is not intended to serve as a replacement for professional medical advice. Any use of the information in this book is at the reader's discretion. The author and the publisher specifically disclaim any and all liability arising directly or indirectly from the use or application of any information contained in this book. A health care professional should be consulted regarding your specific situation.

All brand-name products cited in this book are the registered trademark properties of their respective companies.

ISBN: 0-471-34798-1

Printed in the United States of America

10   9   8   7   6   5   4   3   2   1

Table of Contents

Introduction 5
How to Use This Book 8

McDonald's 15
Burger King 25
KFC 35
Pizza Hut 45
Wendy's 55
Taco Bell 65
Hardee's 75
Subway 85
Domino's 95
Dairy Queen 105
Little Caesar's 115
Arby's 125

Appendixes

Hamburgers Ranked by Calories, Fat,
   and Sodium 135
French Fries Ranked by Weight, Calories,
   Fat, and Sodium 136
Shakes Ranked by Size, Calories, and Fat 138
Soft Drinks vs. Milk: A Comparison of Nutrients . 139
Worldwide Sales, 1997 140
Franchise Fees 141
Bibliography 143

Notice: Consult a Health Care Professional

Because individual cases and needs vary, readers are advised to seek the guidance of a licensed physician, registered dietitian, or other health care professional before making changes in their prescribed health care regimens. This book is intended for informational purposes only and is not for use as an alternative to appropriate medical care. While every effort has been made to ensure that the information is the most current available, new research findings and menu items, as well as recipe modifications, may invalidate some data.

Introduction

Fast food and restaurant franchising have reshaped America. In a span of 40 years, we now eat half of our food from restaurants, and fast food accounts for 65 percent of all restaurant sales. On any given day, over 18 million people eat at U.S. fast food locations that offer limited, standardized menus of mostly hamburgers, french fries, and soft drinks.

Combo meals containing over 1,000 calories began to dominate fast food menu boards in 1988. That's when fast food operators discovered they could sell more food to more customers and make more money by promoting easy-to-order meal combinations as "more food for your money."

Unfortunately, fast food chains have been combining menu items and adding up the prices for us, but nobody's been tallying up the fat and the calories—until we notice that our clothes are too tight, we need to wear a larger size, or our stomach hangs over our belt. We've all been putting on pounds because many of the popular combo meals add up to more than 1,000 calories per meal.

For inactive people, 1,000 calories can be more than half the amount of energy our bodies need for an entire day, and those excess calories slowly accumulate as fat on our bodies. Eating more calories than our body needs each day and not being physically active are two slow-but-sure ways to gain weight.

But being overweight is not the only concern of eating more fast food. When many of the calories come from fat, especially saturated fat, we increase our risk of developing heart disease over many years. And by routinely eating at fast food locations, we seldom get enough of the fresh fruits and vegetables that can reduce our risk of cancer and lower high blood pressure.

Still, we like the convenience, speed, price, and the taste of fast food. We simply don't have the time or the knowledge to quickly and easily order lower-calorie, lower-fat meal combinations even though we want to eat better and restaurants sell foods that can be combined into meals that are better for us.

This pocket guide contains 48 different lower-calorie, lower-fat meals from the top twelve fast food chains for quick and easy ordering at the drive-thru window or the walk-up counter. Each meal lists what to order and the amount, then "does the math" by totaling the calories, nutrients, and dietary exchanges for the entire meal. And to keep the fun in fast food, each meal page alternates with a page of fast food trivia and a healthy eating tip to help sustain better eating habits.

Each smart combo meal totals 700 calories or less. That's one-third of the 2,100 calories needed each day by some adults. Less than 30 percent of the calories in these meals come from fat. The calories, fat, saturated fat, dietary fiber, and sodium are totaled from nutrition data provided by each fast food chain.

A range of target values for key nutrients is repeated on each meal page as a comparison with the total nutrients a better meal might have. These target values are based upon diets of 2,000 to 2,500 calories per day established for food labels by the Food and Drug Administration. The ranges are one-third of those Daily Values and assume that a meal is one of three meals eaten in a day.

Of course, the total calories needed in one day depends upon your gender, age, health status, and activity level, so your requirements may be higher or lower by several hundred calories for a day. The purpose of target values is simply to compare the totals for a specific meal with reasonable target amounts.

Smart Fast Food Meals makes it easy for you to order lower-calorie and lower-fat fast food meals because the foods and the exact amounts to order are at your fingertips. Put this pocket guide to good use by keeping it in your purse, a pocket, or the glove compartment of your car or truck. Enjoy your favorite fast food—without becoming supersized!

How to Use This Book

You've got to have a plan when you order fast food meals or you'll wind up ordering the latest fast food promotion or combo meal which appeals to your wallet but may risk your health. Remember, it's up to you to make better food choices, so plan your order before you drive up to that fast food window or walk up to the counter. Be sure you're getting a fast food meal of less than 700 calories and less than 30 percent calories from fat by following these simple steps:

- Use this book when you go to a fast food restaurant. It fits into a purse, pocket, or glove compartment.
- Select a smart combo meal from the restaurant of your choice.
- Order the food and the amounts listed.
- Compare the calorie and fat totals for each meal with the target values. You'll get a better understanding of the amounts of some of the key nutrients your body needs each day.
- Check out the fast food trivia and healthy eating tips offered with each smart meal.
- Enjoy your smart fast food meal knowing that you're taking control and eating better for a healthier, happier life.

Here are a few more pointers about choosing better fast food meals:

- You can't go wrong substituting skim milk for a regular soft drink listed with any of the meals in this book. Meals with diet soft drinks also benefit from switching to skim milk by adding other nutrients plus about 85 calories per 8-ounce carton. The added protein and carbohydrate in skim milk may help stave off overeating at your next meal.

  Milk is one of the greatest sources of calcium in the American diet, but only when we drink it. Milk is not as profitable a beverage to sell as soft drinks, so fast food operators don't promote milk or combine it in their combo meals. They do want your business, however, so they respond to customers requests for skim milk. See page 139 for a comparison of the nutrients in milk versus regular and diet soft drinks.

- Carbohydrate counting is a new way for people with diabetes to match their meal plan with fast food meals. All readers can use this information to get an overview of the total servings of carbohydrates, protein, and fat in each fast food meal.

  As we age and gain weight, we may develop diabetes, which is controlled through diet plus medication. This means eating specific amounts of foods from groups called dietary exchanges. Carbohydrate counting combines the starch/bread, fruit, and milk exchange lists together as one carbohydrate group. It can be an easier way for people with diabetes to plan their meals and control the sugar in their bloodstream.

Early symptoms of diabetes may include excessive thirst, frequency of urination, and nighttime urination. If you are experiencing even one of these symptoms, make an appointment with a doctor for an evaluation. Undiagnosed diabetes can lead to other health problems, especially if untreated.

◆ Know what foods you're missing when you eat at limited-menu fast food restaurants and figure out a way to include them in another meal at home or a full-menu restaurant. Here are a few foods you won't see at a typical fast food chain:

Fresh, canned, or frozen fruit. An apple, an orange, a banana, a bunch of grapes, a slice of watermelon, cantaloupe, pineapple, strawberries, kiwi, blueberries, a peach, mango, plums, apricots, cherries. What could be easier, healthier, and more refreshing than a simple serving of fruit or fruit juice?

Fresh, canned, or frozen vegetables. You've heard these words before, "Eat your vegetables." Call it mother's intuition, but studies confirm she's been right all along. People who eat at least five servings of fruits and vegetables a day have half the risk of getting cancer. (A serving is 1/2 cup cooked or 1 cup raw.) And eating more vegetables may also help control blood pressure.

It's worth your effort to add a veggie or two to your next meal. Mull over these possibilities: asparagus, tomatoes, onion, carrots, green beans, spinach, rutabaga, broccoli, corn, celery, green and red peppers, mushrooms, cauliflower, sugar snap peas, zucchini, lima beans, cabbage, sweet potatoes, beets, cucumber, peas. Does this list make you realize you're missing something when you eat only fast food?

- ◆ You're still hungry? These smart fast food meals are planned for the person who needs no more than 2,500 calories per day. If you find you're still hungry, you may need to take a closer look at your personal caloric requirements, or consider that you've become used to overeating fast food and it's difficult to cut back to smaller amounts. If your daily activity level is high or your body is more muscle than fat, carefully choose additional lower fat foods based on nutrition charts each fast food restaurant provides. Snack on a few graham crackers, a piece of fruit, or a bagel with jam (skip the cream cheese) to sustain you to the next regular meal.
- ◆ Pay attention to promotions. You're getting smart about fast food when you recognize that advertising and promotion by fast food restaurants doesn't nec-

essarily coincide with what foods and what amounts your body actually needs. Take advantage of the convenience and taste of fast foods, but learn the difference between what foods you need and what advertising says you should buy.
- ◆ Consider that many Americans today eat cheap, eat fast, eat alone, and eat more. That awareness is the beginning step in eating smarter and healthier. Use this book to make better food choices, share eating time with another, and be thankful for the abundance of food that many Americans enjoy.

Hamburgers

Five of the top twelve fast food chains specialize in hamburgers and operate over 46,000 restaurants throughout the world. By 1993, there was one fast food hamburger place for every 10,000 residents in the United States.

Red meat such as hamburger continues to be an important part of the American diet, but its consumption has been declining in the United States since about 1976. Boneless chicken products developed in the 1970s appeal to restaurant operators and eaters alike who don't want the mess of discarded chicken bones.

Health concerns have also been a factor in this shift from beef to chicken. The saturated fat in meat has been implicated in the development of heart disease, and a 3-ounce hamburger patty contains more saturated fat than the same amount of chicken.

Fast food hamburger chains added chicken items to their menus and continue to capture 35 percent of all fast food restaurant sales.

McDonald's
FAST FACTS

Ranked #1 in sales

Parent company: McDonald's Corporation, publicly traded on the New York Stock Exchange as MCD

Headquarters: Oak Brook, IL

Year founded: 1948 in San Bernardino, CA; incorporated in 1955 by Ray Kroc

Founders: Brothers Richard "Dick" and Maurice "Mac" MacDonald

Worldwide sales: $33,638,000,000

Number of stores worldwide: 23,132

One patent: The McDonald's high chair

One memorable ad campaign: "Look for the Golden Arches"

Charitable giving: The Ronald McDonald House Charities provide housing near major hospitals for families of hospitalized children.

Good**for**You!

Bring back the word "small" to McDonald's! To satisfy your craving for french fries, say "small" when you order fries. You'll get the least amount of fat and calories in an order of fries—but you gotta say "small"!

Trivia

In 1948, Dick and Mac MacDonald increased business at their California drive-in restaurants by reducing the number of menu items to hamburgers, fries, and milk shakes. Their plan was to attract families, not teenagers, so they eliminated the carhops, the seating, the jukeboxes, and the telephones!

McDonald's
SMART COMBO MEAL

- **1 Hamburger**
- **1 small order french fries**
- **1 medium regular soft drink (21 oz.)**

Nutrients	Target Values for one meal*	Approx. Values for this meal
Calories	666–833	680
Total Fat	22–27 gm.	19 gm.
Saturated Fat	7–8 gm.	5 gm.
% Calories From Fat	30%	25%
Dietary Fiber	8–10 gm.	4 gm.
Sodium	<800 mg.	735 mg.

Dietary Exchanges for this meal:

Carbohydrate	Vegetable	Meat	Fat
8	0	1 medium fat	3

*Based on 2,000 to 2,500 calories per day

Good **for** You!

What is the worst possible thing that can happen if you say "hold the mayo" when you order a grilled chicken sandwich? You'll get a funny look? You'll have to wait 20 seconds? It won't drip on your clothes like it usually does? Go ahead, say it: "Hold the mayo!"

Trivia

Stock in the McDonald's Corporation has been traded on the New York Stock Exchange (NYSE) since 1965. McDonald's is now one of the 30 companies that make up the Dow Jones Industrial Average, a leading economic indicator.

McDonald's
SMART COMBO MEAL

- 1 Grilled Chicken Deluxe Sandwich (hold the mayo!)
- 1 small order french fries
- 1 small regular soft drink (16 oz.)

Nutrients	Target Values for one meal*	Approx. Values for this meal
Calories	666–833	660
Total Fat	22–27 gm.	15 gm.
Saturated Fat	7–8 gm.	2.5 gm.
% Calories From Fat	30%	20%
Dietary Fiber	8–10 gm.	5 gm.
Sodium	<800 mg.	1,080 mg.

Dietary Exchanges for this meal:

Carbohydrate	Vegetable	Meat	Fat
7	0	3 very lean	2

*Based on 2,000 to 2,500 calories per day

Good**for**You!

Cookies and milk have always made a great taste combo! Make sure the milk is skim or 1 percent and eat only one package of McDonaldland cookies. If you add fresh fruit to this meal, it's still less than 700 calories.

Trivia

In 1964, owner and president Ray Kroc thought customers would enjoy the burger sandwich that he often ate for lunch. He added a slice of grilled pineapple with two slices of cheese and called it the "Hulaburger." Needless to say, it flopped when it was introduced, but confirmed the importance of test marketing. (Hey, nobody's perfect!)

McDonald's
SMART COMBO MEAL

- 1 Hamburger
- 1 package McDonaldland cookies
- 1 carton 1% or skim milk (8 oz.)

Nutrients	Target Values for one meal*	Approx. Values for this meal
Calories	666–833	540
Total Fat	22–27 gm.	16.5 gm.
Saturated Fat	7–8 gm.	6 gm.
% Calories From Fat	30%	28%
Dietary Fiber	8–10 gm.	3 gm.
Sodium	<800 mg.	885 mg.

Dietary Exchanges for this meal:

Carbohydrate	Vegetable	Meat	Fat
5 1/2	0	1 medium fat	2

*Based on 2,000 to 2,500 calories per day

Good**for**You!

Look and feel like a kid again when you order kid-size portions. Don't worry about anyone asking for your I.D. Fast food operators are interested in your money, not your age—or your health!

Trivia

No other fast food restaurant has changed America's eating habits more than McDonald's. Do you remember when these foods were first introduced?

Big Mac 1968
Egg McMuffin 1973
Chicken McNuggets 1980
Prepackaged salads 1986

McDonald's
SMART COMBO MEAL

- Chicken McNuggets (4 pieces) with honey, barbecue sauce, or sweet 'n sour sauce
- 1 Strawberry Sundae
- 1 small regular soft drink (16 oz.)

Nutrients	Target Values for one meal*	Approx. Values for this meal
Calories	666–833	680
Total Fat	22–27 gm.	18 gm.
Saturated Fat	7–8 gm.	7.5 gm.
% Calories From Fat	30%	24%
Dietary Fiber	8–10 gm.	0 gm.
Sodium	<800 mg.	650 mg.

Dietary Exchanges for this meal:

Carbohydrate	Vegetable	Meat	Fat
7 1/2	0	2 medium fat	1 1/2

*Based on 2,000 to 2,500 calories per day

A Fast History of Franchising

As early as the 1920s, Howard Johnson's ice cream parlors offered consistent food quality at readily recognizable locations—a marketing concept that still holds true today. He persuaded others to build their own restaurants, sell his menu items, then pay him a percentage of their sales. The Howard Johnson name and image could guarantee customer traffic, sales, and profits. Restaurant franchising was born!

A&W Rootbeer stands were early franchise operations, but franchising didn't gain momentum until the 1950s. Walk-up stores like Dairy Queen introduced soft-serve ice cream, and the franchising boom took off into the 1960s. Potential small business owners saw franchising as their opportunity to operate a proven and profitable restaurant with a relatively small investment.

It's still possible to become a millionaire by owning and operating a fast food restaurant; you just need to start out with more money!

Burger King
FAST FACTS

Ranked #2 in sales

Parent company: Diageo, London, UK

Headquarters: Miami, FL

Year founded: 1954

Founders: James McLamore and David Edgerton; sold in 1967 to the Pillsbury Company, which is now a division of Diageo

Worldwide sales: $9,800,000,000

Number of stores worldwide: about 9,400

One patent: A condiment dispenser

One memorable ad campaign: "Have It Your Way" (Hold the pickles, hold the lettuce, special orders don't upset us...)

Charitable giving: The Burger King Foundation assists local franchise restaurants with a variety of education programs in their communities.

Good**for**You!

In spite of the hype about getting more value for your money, the truth is that you spend less money when you order less food. It's not a value if you gain weight or develop heart disease from regularly eating fat-filled fast food. Go back to eating smaller meals again.

Trivia

In 1954, the price of a Burger King hamburger was only 18 cents. Unfortunately, that was 3 cents more than the price of a McDonald's hamburger, and Burger King has been playing catch-up with the number one in fast food sales ever since!

Burger King
SMART COMBO MEAL

- **1 Hamburger**
- **1 medium Vanilla Shake (10 oz.)**

Nutrients	Target Values for one meal*	Approx. Values for this meal
Calories	666–833	640
Total Fat	22–27 gm.	21.5 gm.
Saturated Fat	7–8 gm.	9.5 gm.
% Calories From Fat	30%	30%
Dietary Fiber	8–10 gm.	2 gm.
Sodium	<800 mg.	765 mg.

Dietary Exchanges for this meal:

Carbohydrate	Vegetable	Meat	Fat
5 1/2	0	4 medium fat	0

*Based on 2,000 to 2,500 calories per day

Good **for** You!

Choosing a regular soft drink instead of diet is one way to get calories without fat. Soft drink calories provide only energy and may help you feel full sooner. But there are no other nutrients in soft drinks, so they are often referred to as empty calories.

Trivia

During the 1970s, some Burger King franchise operations did not follow the standards set by the parent company. A former McDonald's executive was hired to improve food quality and consistency, and required new Burger King franchise owners to live within an hour's drive of their restaurants.

Burger King
SMART COMBO MEAL

- **1 B.K. Broiler Chicken Sandwich (hold the mayo!)**
- **1 small regular soft drink (16 oz.)**

Nutrients	Target Values for one meal*	Approx. Values for this meal
Calories	666–833	650
Total Fat	22–27 gm.	16.5 gm.
Saturated Fat	7–8 gm.	4.5 gm.
% Calories From Fat	30%	23%
Dietary Fiber	8–10 gm.	2 gm.
Sodium	<800 mg.	750 mg.

Dietary Exchanges for this meal:

Carbohydrate	Vegetable	Meat	Fat
5	0	4 lean	1

*Based on 2,000 to 2,500 calories per day

Good **for** You!

Slow down when you're eating! Pay attention to feeling full as you eat to keep from overeating. And watch out for those inattentive drivers who eat while driving!

Trivia

An Elvis sighting was reported at a Burger King in Kalamazoo, Michigan. Where else would "the King" eat?

Burger King
SMART COMBO MEAL

- **1 Whopper Jr. (hold the mayo!)**
- **1 medium regular soft drink (22 oz.)**

Nutrients	Target Values for one meal*	Approx. Values for this meal
Calories	666–833	600
Total Fat	22–27 gm.	12 gm.
Saturated Fat	7–8 gm.	7 gm.
% Calories From Fat	30%	18%
Dietary Fiber	8–10 gm.	2 gm.
Sodium	<800 mg.	750 mg.

Dietary Exchanges for the meal:

Carbohydrate	Vegetable	Meat	Fat
6	0	3 lean	1/2

*Based on 2,000 to 2,500 calories per day

Good **for** You!

Ordering a lower-calorie, lower-fat meal improves your eating style in a small, gradual way. Cutting back on the amount you eat at a fast food place is just the reverse of how you added those calories (and pounds) in the first place. Downsize your meal, so you won't be "super-sized!"

Trivia

When Chicken Tenders were first introduced in 1986, they were so popular that Burger King couldn't keep up with the demand and had to stop the introductory advertising campaign early.

Burger King
SMART COMBO MEAL

- **Chicken Tenders (8 pieces)**
- **Sweet & Sour Dipping Sauce (1 oz.)**
- **1 medium regular soft drink (22 oz.)**

Nutrients	Target Values for one meal*	Approx. Values for this meal
Calories	666–833	675
Total Fat	22–27 gm.	22 gm.
Saturated Fat	7–8 gm.	7 gm.
% Calories From Fat	30%	29%
Dietary Fiber	8–10 gm.	1 gm.
Sodium	<800 mg.	1,015 mg.

Dietary Exchanges for this meal:

Carbohydrate	Vegetable	Meat	Fat
6	0	3 medium fat	1/2

*Based on 2,000 to 2,500 calories per day

Secrets to Success

What does it take for one restaurant in a chain to be successful? Think of VATS to attract customers to fast and familiar food: Visibility, Access, Traffic, and Signs.

Potential fast food owners look for prime locations along major highways, then seek approvals for large signs and convenient driveways from local city officials. Land is often the largest initial expense of stand-alone fast food restaurants, costing many times more than the actual building and kitchen equipment.

When Ray Kroc built a McDonald's restaurant, he deliberately sought less expensive land in the middle of a block and not at the intersection. McDonald's stores are usually situated on lots for easy entrance and exit by cars.

Colonel Sanders required a daily traffic count of at least 16,000 cars (preferably heading home for dinner) before approving a location for Kentucky Fried Chicken. His protégé Dave Thomas—who later went on to found Wendy's—patented the red-and-white revolving bucket that readily identified the first KFC locations.

KFC

FAST FACTS

Ranked #3 in sales

Parent company formed in 1997: Tricon Global Restaurants, Inc., a publicly held company traded on the New York Stock Exchange as YUM (includes Pizza Hut and Taco Bell); **Parent company name before October 1997:** PepsiCo Foodservice, Inc.

Headquarters: Louisville, KY

Year founded: 1955 as Kentucky Fried Chicken

Founder: Harland "Colonel" Sanders

Worldwide sales: $8,200,000,000

Number of stores worldwide: 10,237

One patent: Chicken frying equipment

One memorable tag line: "Finger lickin' good"

Charitable giving: Churches, Salvation Army, schools

Good **for** You!

An order of mashed potatoes and gravy from KFC has fewer calories and fat than an order of french fries from any other major fast food chain. And because you eat them with a spoon, fork, or spork, they slow you down to enjoy your meal. Mashed potatoes: a speed bump in the fast lane of this American life!

Trivia

By 1970, Kentucky Fried Chicken had created 130 millionaires—franchise owners who had each invested an average of $68,000 to start a fried chicken and biscuits take-out operation!

KFC

SMART COMBO MEAL

- 1 Tender Roast Chicken breast with skin
- 1 order Mashed Potatoes & Gravy
- 1 order Corn-on-the-Cob
- 1 small regular soft drink (16 oz.)

Nutrients	Target Values for one meal*	Approx. Values for this meal
Calories	666–833	670
Total Fat	22–27 gm.	18.5 gm.
Saturated Fat	7–8 gm.	4 gm.
% Calories From Fat	30%	25%
Dietary Fiber	8–10 gm.	4 gm.
Sodium	<800 mg.	1,305 mg.

Dietary Exchanges for this meal:

Carbohydrate	Vegetables	Meat	Fat
6	0	5 lean	0

*Based on 2,000 to 2,500 calories per day

Good**for**You!

At mealtime, savor just one or two small pieces of chicken, and eat breads, vegetables, pasta, and potatoes prepared without extra butter or margarine. If you're hungry for more, ask for an order of potatoes instead of the biscuit often added by KFC.

Trivia

Founder Colonel Sanders began his first restaurant in 1929 by frying chicken for customers in the back room of his gas station in Corbin, Kentucky. Hmmm! Wonder what kind of oil he used?

KFC

SMART COMBO MEAL

- **2 Original Recipe Drumsticks (Say "No biscuit")**
- **1 order Corn-on-the-Cob**
- **1 small regular soft drink (16 oz.)**

Nutrients	Target Values for one meal*	Approx. Values for this meal
Calories	666–833	580
Total Fat	22–27 gm.	19.5 gm.
Saturated Fat	7–8 gm.	4 gm.
% Calories From Fat	30%	30%
Dietary Fiber	8–10 gm.	2 gm.
Sodium	<800 mg.	880 mg.

Dietary Exchanges for this meal:

Carbohydrate	Vegetables	Meat	Fat
5 1/2	0	3 medium fat	0

*Based on 2,000 to 2,500 calories per day

Good**for**You!

Look for and order foods with high dietary fiber like corn-on-the-cob, potato wedges, baked potato with skin, refried beans, and baked beans. You'll find these at KFC, Taco Bell, Wendy's, Hardee's, and Arby's. Dietary fiber may reduce the risk of both cancer and heart disease—as long as you skip the butter, sour cream, and cheese offered with them!

Trivia

At the age of 65, Colonel Sanders traveled from city to city in the 1950s demonstrating his chicken cooking procedure at restaurants and convincing owners to buy a few pieces of equipment and pay him 5 cents for every order they served. He would stay on a few days making sure sales of his chicken caught on, often sleeping in his car.

KFC

SMART COMBO MEAL

- ◆ 1 order Colonel's Crispy Strips (3 pieces)
- ◆ 1 order Potatoes & Gravy
- ◆ 1 order Corn-on-the-Cob
- ◆ 1 small regular soft drink (16 oz.)

Nutrients	Target Values for one meal*	Approx. Values for this meal
Calories	666–833	680
Total Fat	22–27 gm.	23.5 gm.
Saturated Fat	7–8 gm.	5 gm.
% Calories From Fat	30%	31%
Dietary Fiber	8–10 gm.	7 gm.
Sodium	<800 mg.	1,130 mg.

Dietary Exchanges for this meal:

Carbohydrate	Vegetables	Meat	Fat
6 1/2	0	2 1/2 high fat	0

*Based on 2,000 to 2,500 calories per day

Good **for** You!

Salt is a food preservative and seasoning used throughout the world. However, about one-third of Americans are sensitive to salt, which means it causes their blood pressure to increase. High blood pressure harms blood vessels, lungs, heart, and kidneys. Salt is used extensively in fast food, so carefully check the nutrition brochures and order lower-salt foods.

Trivia

The first American fast food operation in China was Kentucky Fried Chicken. It opened in Beijing in 1987 and quickly became the top-selling KFC store, selling $3 million worth of fried chicken in one year.

KFC

SMART COMBO MEAL

- **1 Value BBQ Chicken Sandwich**
- **1 order Potato Wedges**
- **1 small regular soft drink (16 oz.)**

Nutrients	Target Values for one meal*	Approx. Values for this meal
Calories	666–833	690
Total Fat	22–27 gm.	21 gm.
Saturated Fat	7–8 gm.	5 gm.
% Calories From Fat	30%	27%
Dietary Fiber	8–10 gm.	7 gm.
Sodium	<800 mg.	1,550 mg.

Dietary Exchanges for this meal:

Carbohydrate	Vegetables	Meat	Fat
6	0	1 1/2 lean	3

*Based on 2,000 to 2,500 calories per day

Soft**Drinks**

Carbonated beverages are called soft drinks or soda or pop to most of us, but they're known as popular and profitable to fast food operators. Soft drinks contain sugar, water, and unique flavorings, making them relatively inexpensive to produce. The biggest cost in the soft drink industry is advertising and promotions.

Soft drink manufacturers and fast food chains enjoy alliances that are mutually beneficial. A beverage company may install their soft drink dispensers in every restaurant in a chain as a way to secure the sale of its brand. The chain restaurant in return enjoys more customer traffic and sales due to the national advertising by the soft drink company. More soft drink sales mean higher profits for both businesses.

In the United States, soft drink consumption increased from 13.6 gallons per person per year in 1960 to 47.5 gallons per person in 1990. At the same time, milk consumption declined to 24.5 gallons per person, resulting in the demise of 7.5 million milk cows and tens of thousands of dairy farms.

Pizza Hut
FAST FACTS

Ranked #4 in sales

Parent company formed in 1997: Tricon Global Restaurants, Inc., a publicly held company traded on the New York Stock Exchange as YUM (includes KFC Corporation and Taco Bell); **Parent company name before October 1997:** PepsiCo Foodservice, Inc.

Headquarters: Dallas, TX

Year founded: 1958

Founders: Brothers Dan and Frank Carney and John Bender

Worldwide sales: $7,300,000,000

Number of stores worldwide: 14,400

One interesting patent: A breadstick cutter

One memorable ad campaign: "Makin' it great!"

Charitable giving: BOOK IT! National Reading Incentive Program encouraging higher literacy among young people

Good **for** You!

Cutting back on fat and calories at Pizza Hut is as easy as remembering what type of crust to order. Say "Thin 'N Crispy" for the lowest amount of fat in a crust at Pizza Hut.

Trivia

Many restaurant operators dream of starting a successful restaurant by using their favorite recipes from mama. But the Carney brothers asked their mama instead for $600 to start a pizza parlor in 1958 in Wichita, Kansas. Mama Carney's money launched the world's largest pizza chain, Pizza Hut.

Pizza Hut
SMART COMBO MEAL

- **3 slices of a medium Thin 'n Crispy Ham Pizza**
- **1 Diet Pepsi**

Nutrients	Target Values for one meal*	Approx. Values for this meal
Calories	666–833	575
Total Fat	22–27 gm.	18 gm.
Saturated Fat	7–8 gm.	9 gm.
% Calories From Fat	30%	28%
Dietary Fiber	8–10 gm.	3 gm.
Sodium	<800 mg.	1,710 mg.

Dietary Exchanges for this meal:

Carbohydrate	Vegetable	Meat	Fat
4 1/2	0	2 1/2 lean	2

*Based on 2,000 to 2,500 calories per day

Good **for** You!

Ordering a veggie pizza with bell peppers, onions, mushrooms, and tomato sauce is an easy way to cut back on saturated fat and increase the amount of dietary fiber—two ways to improve the health of your heart.

Trivia

Fast food chains often adapt the foods and seasonings of other countries when they build restaurants overseas. Pizza Hut toppings include sardines and tuna in Moscow, curry flavors in Asia and Australia, and corned beef and Canadian bacon in Hong Kong.

Pizza Hut
SMART COMBO MEAL

- **2 slices of a medium Thin 'n Crispy Veggie Lover's Pizza**
- **2 Breadsticks with Dipping Sauce**
- **1 Diet Pepsi**

Nutrients	Target Values for one meal*	Approx. Values for this meal
Calories	666–833	635
Total Fat	22–27 gm.	20.5 gm.
Saturated Fat	7–8 gm.	6 gm.
% Calories From Fat	30%	29%
Dietary Fiber	8–10 gm.	8 gm.
Sodium	<800 mg.	1,460 mg.

Dietary Exchanges for this meal:

Carbohydrate	Vegetable	Meat	Fat
5 1/2	2	0	3 1/2

*Based on 2,000 to 2,500 calories per day

Good**for**You!

Spaghetti with meatless marinara sauce from Pizza Hut comes with two pieces of garlic bread—a combo that automatically adds more fat and calories than you want to eat. It's up to you to ask to substitute a lower-fat breadstick, so do it!

Trivia

Just about everybody knows what most Pizza Huts look like: red-roofed, one-story, brick and wood buildings established in 1973 as the standard design and part of the Pizza Hut logo. Quick visual recognition of a fast food location helps increase customer traffic and sales.

Pizza Hut
SMART COMBO MEAL

- **1 order Spaghetti with Marinara Sauce (meatless)**
- **1 Breadstick with Dipping Sauce (in place of garlic bread)**
- **1 Diet Pepsi**

Nutrients	Target Values for one meal*	Approx. Values for this meal
Calories	666–833	655
Total Fat	22–27 gm.	10.5 gm.
Saturated Fat	7–8 gm.	2 gm.
% Calories From Fat	30%	14%
Dietary Fiber	8–10 gm.	9.5 gm.
Sodium	<800 mg.	1,100 mg.

Dietary Exchanges for this meal:

Carbohydrate	Vegetable	Meat	Fat
7 1/2	1	0	1

*Based on 2,000 to 2,500 calories per day

Good **for** You!

Bring along a buddy or two when you eat out at a pizza place. Take your time to talk more and eat less—and feel more satisfied after sharing a meal.

Trivia

The founders of Pizza Hut sold more than pizza. In 1959, one year after opening their first pizza parlor, they began selling franchise rights to other restaurant operators. By 1966, there were 145 Pizza Huts selling pizza and paying franchise fees to the original founders—making them a lot of dough!

Pizza Hut
SMART COMBO MEAL

- **2 slices of a medium Hand Tossed–Style Pepperoni Pizza**
- **1 small regular Pepsi (12 oz.)**

Nutrients	Target Values for one meal*	Approx. Values for this meal
Calories	666–833	670
Total Fat	22–27 gm.	18 gm.
Saturated Fat	7–8 gm.	8 gm.
% Calories From Fat	30%	24%
Dietary Fiber	8–10 gm.	6 gm.
Sodium	<800 mg.	1,515 mg.

Dietary Exchanges for this meal:

Carbohydrate	Vegetable	Meat	Fat
6 1/2	0	1 high fat	1 1/2

*Based on 2,000 to 2,500 calories per day

Advertising

Ad agencies love fast food. Every national restaurant chain depends upon television advertising, and that means fierce competition between ad agencies to earn millions of dollars by creating even one ad campaign. McDonald's spent $75 million promoting just the Arch Deluxe.

Fast food restaurants review and change ad agencies to spark interest and increase sales. Wendy's first ad campaign featured an animated, red-haired, pigtailed "Wendy" dancing with hamburgers.

In 1983, Wendy's TV commercials used humor in a three-way burger battle with McDonald's and Burger King that promoted the quality and freshness of its hamburgers. The following year, the same ad agency created Wendy's famous "Where's the beef?" commercial quoted by presidential candidate Walter Mondale. It was voted the most popular commercial in America in 1984.

Wendy's
FAST FACTS

Ranked #5 in sales

Parent company: Wendy's International, Inc., which is publicly held and traded on the New York Stock Exchange as WEN

Headquarters: Dublin, OH

Year founded: 1969

Founder: R. David "Dave" Thomas

Worldwide sales: $5,226,000,000

Number of stores worldwide: 5,206

One interesting patent: Griddle-mounted hot dog turner with lift-off detachable drive unit

One memorable ad campaign: "Where's the beef?"

Charitable giving: The Dave Thomas Foundation for Adoption

Good **for** You!

Every fast food joint has some kind of chicken sandwich, but you've got to say "grilled" to get a chicken sandwich that hasn't been deep-fried and loaded with more fat. Squeeze a packet or two of mustard on that chicken for added flavor without the calories or fat.

Trivia

In 1979, Wendy's was the first fast food chain to add a salad bar and became the third most popular chain restaurant by adding chicken sandwiches and baked potatoes to its menu. Wendy's introduced millions of fast food customers to pocket bread when it began offering Fresh Stuffed Pitas.

Wendy's
SMART COMBO MEAL

- **1 Grilled Chicken Sandwich**
- **1 small order French Fries**
- **1 small regular soft drink (8 oz.)**

Nutrients	Target Values for one meal*	Approx. Values for this meal
Calories	666–833	670
Total Fat	22–27 gm.	21 gm.
Saturated Fat	7–8 gm.	3.5 gm.
% Calories From Fat	30%	28%
Dietary Fiber	8–10 gm.	5 gm.
Sodium	<800 mg.	885 mg.

Dietary Exchanges for this meal:

Carbohydrate	Vegetable	Meat	Fat
6	0	2 1/2 very lean	3

*Based on 2,000 to 2,500 calories per day

Good **for** You!

It takes two hands to handle a pocket sandwich stuffed with veggies and chicken chunks. That's another good reason to skip an order of french fries. When you finish, give yourself a pat on the back for eating this lower-fat, lower-calorie meal!

Trivia

Founder Dave Thomas credits part of his success to his determination to overcome a tough childhood, and in 1992 he established a foundation that promotes adoption. It works to create national awareness of the joys of adoption, including a petition drive for an adoption postage stamp.

Wendy's
SMART COMBO MEAL

- **1 Chicken Caesar Fresh Stuffed Pita (with dressing)**
- **1 medium regular soft drink (12 oz.)**

Nutrients	Target Values for one meal*	Approx. Values for this meal
Calories	666–833	625
Total Fat	22–27 gm.	18 gm.
Saturated Fat	7–8 gm.	5 gm.
% Calories From Fat	30%	26%
Dietary Fiber	8–10 gm.	4 gm.
Sodium	<800 mg.	1,335 mg.

Dietary Exchanges for this meal:

Carbohydrate	Vegetable	Meat	Fat
5 1/2	0	3 1/2 very lean	2 1/2

*Based on 2,000 to 2,500 calories per day

Good**for**You!

You can watch your calories and still enjoy the taste of chili and a Frosty by ordering the smallest size. Portion size means everything when you're watching your calories and your weight, not how much money you'll save by ordering a bigger portion.

Trivia

Founder and high-school dropout Dave Thomas had already achieved millionaire status as a successful restaurant operator with Kentucky Fried Chicken when he started this new restaurant venture in 1969. He had only a local chain in mind that would create summer jobs for his own children. By 1996, Wendy's had grown to 42,000 employees worldwide.

Wendy's
SMART COMBO MEAL

- 1 large Chili (12 oz.)
- 2 packets saltine crackers (4 crackers)
- 1 small Frosty (12 oz.)

Nutrients	Target Values for one meal*	Approx. Values for this meal
Calories	666–833	690
Total Fat	22–27 gm.	19 gm.
Saturated Fat	7–8 gm.	8.5 gm.
% Calories From Fat	30%	25%
Dietary Fiber	8–10 gm.	7 gm.
Sodium	<800 mg.	1,580 mg.

Dietary Exchanges for this meal:

Carbohydrate	Vegetable	Meat	Fat
6 1/2	0	2 1/2 very lean	1 1/2

*Based on 2,000 to 2,500 calories per day

Good**for**You!

Order soft breadsticks instead of french fries with your meal from Wendy's and you can feel full without all the fat and calories. Now don't go adding butter or margarine to those breadsticks or you've missed the point!

Trivia

Wendy's restaurant chain is consistently rated by consumers as America's favorite hamburger place. People like its homey atmosphere and its wide variety of food choices.

Wendy's
SMART COMBO MEAL

- 1 Jr. Cheeseburger (hold the mayo)
- 2 Soft Breadsticks
- 1 small regular soft drink (8 oz.)

Nutrients	Target Values for one meal*	Approx. Values for this meal
Calories	666–833	670
Total Fat	22–27 gm.	19 gm.
Saturated Fat	7–8 gm.	7 gm.
% Calories From Fat	30%	26%
Dietary Fiber	8–10 gm.	4 gm.
Sodium	<800 mg.	1,340 mg.

Dietary Exchanges for this meal:

Carbohydrate	Vegetable	Meat	Fat
7	0	1 medium fat	1 1/2

*Based on 2,000 to 2,500 calories per day

More Fat **for** Your Money

Value pricing is a tried-and-true strategy for attracting customers, and fast food chains do it well. What could be more American than a deal, and value pricing suggests a deal to fast food customers.

When combo meals were introduced, sales and profits soared for food that was already low priced. Here's a simplified explanation: When customers perceive a greater value in getting more food for their money, they spend more money.

Value pricing of combo meals is a relatively low-risk strategy for the fast food restaurant. It combines one high-cost food item (a sandwich) with two low-cost food items (soft drink and fries) to make one profitable meal. The total amount of each sale increases, the combined food cost is lower, and combo meals simply generate more customer traffic and sales.

Fast food chains also pay attention to competitors' prices. Restaurants with lower food costs and prices such as Taco Bell help keep prices at the burger and chicken places low.

Taco Bell
FAST FACTS

Ranked #6 in sales

Parent company formed in 1997: Tricon Global Restaurants, Inc., a publicly held company traded on the New York Stock Exchange as YUM (includes Pizza Hut and KFC Corporation); **Parent company name before October 1997:** PepsiCo Foodservice, Inc.

Headquarters: Irvine, CA

Year founded: 1962; began in 1952 in San Bernardino, CA, as Taco Tia Restaurant

Founder: Glen Bell

Worldwide sales: $4,900,000,000

Number of stores worldwide: 6,941

One patent: A taco support device

One memorable ad campaign: "Head for the border"

Charitable giving: The Taco Bell Foundation supports Boys and Girls Clubs by establishing TEEN Supreme Centers.

Good **for** You!

Ordering soft shell tacos (tortillas) instead of hard shell automatically cuts back on the amount of fat you eat because hard shells have been fried in fat. Too many crispy hard shells can make you flabby!

Trivia

San Bernardino, California, is the birthplace of two major fast food chains: McDonald's and Taco Bell. In 1946, Glen Bell started with a one-man hot dog stand, then switched to quick-service Mexican food, which was more popular with the local residents.

Taco Bell
SMART COMBO MEAL

- **2 Grilled Steak Soft Tacos**
- **1 medium regular Pepsi (16 oz.)**

Nutrients	Target Values for one meal*	Approx. Values for this meal
Calories	666–833	660
Total Fat	22–27 gm.	20 gm.
Saturated Fat	7–8 gm.	5 gm.
% Calories From Fat	30%	27%
Dietary Fiber	8–10 gm.	4 gm.
Sodium	<800 mg.	2,090 mg.

Dietary Exchanges for this meal:

Carbohydrate	Vegetable	Meat	Fat
6	0	3 lean	2

*Based on 2,000 to 2,500 calories per day

Good **for** You!

One menu item plus a soft drink or skim milk can fill you up as long as you take your time eating. Add an apple, orange, banana, or box of raisins with this meal and you'll still eat less than 700 calories —and feel good about eating, too.

Trivia

PepsiCo, Inc., launched a Mexican food chain in 1975 called Taco Kid to compete against the fast-growing Taco Bell restaurant chain. But when the Taco Kid restaurants failed, PepsiCo simply purchased the entire Taco Bell chain of 868 restaurants in 1978 for nearly $125 million in stock.

Taco Bell
SMART COMBO MEAL

- **1 Grilled Chicken Burrito**
- **1 medium regular Pepsi (16 oz.)**

Nutrients	Target Values for one meal*	Approx. Values for this meal
Calories	666–833	610
Total Fat	22–27 gm.	15 gm.
Saturated Fat	7–8 gm.	4.5 gm.
% Calories From Fat	30%	22%
Dietary Fiber	8–10 gm.	4 gm.
Sodium	<800 mg.	1,430 mg.

Dietary Exchanges for this meal:

Carbohydrate	Vegetable	Meat	Fat
6 1/2	0	1 medium fat	2

*Based on 2,000 to 2,500 calories per day

Good**for**You!

Make a meal of veggies wrapped in a tortilla and you'll be eating nutrients that recent research shows can reduce your risk of cancer. People who eat at least five servings of fruits and vegetables a day are half as likely to get cancer as those who don't eat fruits and vegetables.

Trivia

In 1991, Taco Bell began selling its menu items at three different price levels, becoming the first fast food chain to introduce value pricing, which dominates fast food menu boards today.

Taco Bell
SMART COMBO MEAL

- **1 Veggie Fajita Wrap Supreme**
- **1 medium regular Pepsi (16 oz.)**

Nutrients	Target Values for one meal*	Approx. Values for this meal
Calories	666–833	670
Total Fat	22–27 gm.	22 gm.
Saturated Fat	7–8 gm.	7 gm.
% Calories From Fat	30%	30%
Dietary Fiber	8–10 gm.	3 gm.
Sodium	<800 mg.	1,040 mg.

Dietary Exchanges for this meal:

Carbohydrate	Vegetable	Meat	Fat
6 1/2	1	1 high fat	2 1/2

*Based on 2,000 to 2,500 calories per day

Good **for** You!

When you order a taco salad without the shell from Taco Bell you save yourself from eating an extra 430 calories, which come from the fat-fried shell. Stick with cutting back on fat and calories, and you're on your way to looking and feeling healthier!

Trivia

Founder Glen Bell decided he could make more money by selling tacos in high volume. He developed hard taco shells that were easy and quick to fry at a central kitchen, then packaged and shipped them to his taco stands, where they were stuffed to order.

Taco Bell
SMART COMBO MEAL

- **1 Taco Salad with salsa but without the shell (hold the cheese and sour cream)**
- **1 medium regular Pepsi (16 oz.)**

Nutrients	Target Values for one meal*	Approx. Values for this meal
Calories	666–833	550
Total Fat	22–27 gm.	16 gm.
Saturated Fat	7–8 gm.	7 gm.
% Calories From Fat	30%	26%
Dietary Fiber	8–10 gm.	15 gm.
Sodium	<800 mg.	1,510 mg.

Dietary Exchanges for this meal:

Carbohydrate	Vegetable	Meat	Fat
5	1	2 medium fat	1

*Based on 2,000 to 2,500 calories per day

French**Fries**

Fresh white potatoes were once an important food for Americans. One hundred years ago, American farmers produced enough potatoes to provide nearly 188 pounds per person per year. In 1994, that amount was 90 pounds of potatoes per person, and half of those potatoes are now processed into french fries, potato chips, dehydrated potatoes, and shoestring potatoes.

Before fast food, Americans ate so many fresh potatoes that nutritionists considered them an important source of Vitamins C and B_6. Today, the processing and frying of fresh potatoes into french fries means there is less potato and fewer nutrients per serving but more fat. This change in a food is one example of how fast food affects the health of Americans.

The shift from boiled and mashed potatoes to french fries also changed the way we eat. Potatoes are traditionally served and shared from a common bowl at a family dinner table. French fries and fast foods are served in precise, single-serving portions, making it more acceptable to eat alone.

Hardee's
FAST FACTS

Ranked #7 in sales

Parent company: CKE Restaurants, Inc., Anaheim, CA

Headquarters: Rocky Mount, NC

Year founded: 1960

Founder: Wilbur Hardee

Worldwide sales: $4,900,000,000

Number of stores: 3,056

One interesting patent: control of range hood emissions

One memorable ad campaign: Are you ready for some real food?

Charitable giving: Hardee's Rise and Shine encourages and rewards community service by schoolchildren.

Good**for**You!

Have a plan for ordering a lower-calorie meal before you step up to the counter or drive up to the window. When you decide that you'd rather be thinner than overeat, you're on your way to successful control of your weight.

Trivia

In 1988, Hardee's switched to frying foods in an all-vegetable oil instead of using animal fat. It was the first major chain to announce this change, which means less saturated fat but not a reduction in total fat.

Hardee's
SMART COMBO MEAL

- 1 Hamburger
- 1 small order French Fries
- 1 small Vanilla Cone
- 16 oz. diet soft drink

Nutrients	Target Values for one meal*	Approx. Values for this meal
Calories	666–833	680
Total Fat	22–27 gm.	23 gm.
Saturated Fat	7–8 gm.	7 gm.
% Calories From Fat	30%	30%
Dietary Fiber	8–10 gm.	1 gm.
Sodium	<800 mg.	930 mg.

Dietary Exchanges for this meal:

Carbohydrate	Vegetable	Meat	Fat
6 1/2	0	2 medium fat	2

*Based on 2,000 to 2,500 calories per day

Good**for**You!

You never outgrow your need for milk because milk products contain calcium for keeping bones strong throughout your life. Carefully choose low-fat dairy foods such as milk shakes, puddings, and frozen yogurt—even low-fat cheese—to take care of your body's daily need for calcium.

Trivia

Hardee's restaurant chain grew in 1972 by over 1,000 restaurants when it acquired another fast food chain, Sandy's, and converted those restaurants into Hardee's. To supply its restaurants in the United States, Hardee's operates three production plants and 10 distribution centers.

Hardee's
SMART COMBO MEAL

- **1 Hot Ham 'n' Cheese Sandwich**
- **12 oz. Chocolate Shake**

Nutrients	Target Values for one meal*	Approx. Values for this meal
Calories	666–833	680
Total Fat	22–27 gm.	17 gm.
Saturated Fat	7–8 gm.	9 gm.
% Calories From Fat	30%	23%
Dietary Fiber	8–10 gm.	2 gm.
Sodium	<800 mg.	1,680 mg.

Dietary Exchanges for this meal:

Carbohydrate	Vegetable	Meat	Fat
7	0	2 medium fat	1

*Based on 2,000 to 2,500 calories per day

Good**for**You!

Chicken, mashed potatoes with gravy, and a strawberry sundae can seem like an old-fashioned Sunday meal when you invite someone to eat with you, take the time to sit down to eat, and remember to be thankful for the meal and good company that fills your hunger spot.

Trivia

The first Hardee's restaurant in Rocky Mount, North Carolina, attracted customers with its char-broiled foods prepared on unique cooking equipment that carried away the grease but not the flavor. In 1961, it also attracted two business investors who saw a bright future in a restaurant that was generating $1,000 per week in net profits.

Hardee's
SMART COMBO MEAL

- 1 Chicken Breast
- 1 order Mashed Potatoes
- 1 order Gravy
- 1 Strawberry Sundae
- 16 oz. diet soft drink

Nutrients	Target Values for one meal*	Approx. Values for this meal
Calories	666–833	670
Total Fat	22–27 gm.	17 gm.
Saturated Fat	7–8 gm.	7 gm.
% Calories From Fat	30%	23%
Dietary Fiber	8–10 gm.	3 gm.
Sodium	<800 mg.	1,950 mg.

Dietary Exchanges for this meal:

Carbohydrate	Vegetable	Meat	Fat
6	0	3 medium fat	0

*Based on 2,000 to 2,500 calories per day

Good **for** You!

You're on your way to eating healthier when you're prepared to *not* order a standard combo meal designated by the fast food chain. Take your time to order what you want and feel good about being in control of what you eat.

Trivia

Hardee's dominates the fast food industry today in two important ways: 44 percent of daily sales come from its breakfast business, and Hardee's operates over 1,000 restaurants in small towns with populations of less than 5,000 people.

Hardee's
SMART COMBO MEAL

- 1 Regular Roast Beef Sandwich
- 1 small order Baked Beans
- 1 Strawberry Sundae
- 16 oz. diet soft drink

Nutrients	Target Values for one meal*	Approx. Values for this meal
Calories	666–833	700
Total Fat	22–27 gm.	19 gm.
Saturated Fat	7–8 gm.	7 gm.
% Calories From Fat	30%	24%
Dietary Fiber	8–10 gm.	6 gm.
Sodium	<800 mg.	1,600 mg.

Dietary Exchanges for this meal:

Carbohydrate	Vegetable	Meat	Fat
6 1/2	0	3 lean	1 1/2

*Based on 2,000 to 2,500 calories per day

FastFood**and**Franchising

A savvy restaurant operator can sell more than food. When they specify and patent their successful food service system, they can sell franchising opportunities to others.

Franchised restaurants take advantage of three business practices:

- standardized food and operations for consistent quality and image
- reduced costs due to volume purchasing of everything from food and supplies to building blueprints, advertising, and promotional materials
- mass marketing and merchandising to expand the trade area and increase customer traffic

Franchisees pay building and start-up costs to the parent company plus an initial franchise fee, and a percentage of their monthly restaurant sales as royalty and advertising fees. (See page 141 for a comparison of the top franchise fees.)

Franchisees attend one- or two-week training programs to learn the food operations and service standards in order to be a success. They graduate from programs such as Hamburger U., Whopper College, KFC University, and the College of Pizzarology.

Subway
FAST FACTS

Ranked #8 in sales

Parent company: Doctor's Associates, Inc.

Headquarters: Milford, CT

Year founded: 1965

Founders: Dr. Peter Buck and Fred DeLuca

Worldwide sales: $3,300,000,000

Number of stores worldwide: 13,016

One memorable ad campaign: The Low-Fat Challenge: 7 subs with 6 grams of fat or less

Charitable giving: Established the Micro Investment Lending Enterprise (MILE), based on the principles of the Grameen Bank, to help individuals with small loans found their own businesses.

Good**for**You!

For a quick and easy bonus to your already-low-in-fat submarine sandwich, say, "on whole wheat and hold the cheese" when you order. Whole wheat adds dietary fiber to your diet, and skipping the cheese cuts back on the saturated fat.

Trivia

The cold sandwiches called "subs" enjoy different names in different geographic regions of the United States. Those grinders, hoagies, submarines, poor boys (po'boys), and hero sandwiches all start with a small loaf of Italian or French bread that is layered with sliced meats, cheeses, and condiments and made fresh to order.

Subway
SMART COMBO MEAL

- 1 6-inch Subway Club sandwich on whole wheat bread with lettuce, tomatoes, pickles, green peppers, and olives
- 1 package baked low-fat Potato Crisps (1 1/8 oz.)
- 16 oz. regular soft drink

Nutrients	Target Values for one meal*	Approx. Values for this meal
Calories	666–833	646
Total Fat	22–27 gm.	7 gm.
Saturated Fat	7–8 gm.	2 gm.
% Calories From Fat	30%	10%
Dietary Fiber	8–10 gm.	9 gm.
Sodium	<800 mg.	1,560 mg.

Dietary Exchanges for this meal:

Carbohydrate	Vegetable	Meat	Fat
7 1/2	1	1 1/2 lean	0

*Based on 2,000 to 2,500 calories per day

Good**for**You!

Lettuce, tomatoes, onions, and green peppers are excellent no-fat additions to any sandwich, anytime. Get more flavor in your sandwich when you say "hold the mayo" and ask instead for a sprinkling of oil and vinegar or a big squeeze of mustard.

Trivia

Founders Dr. Peter Buck and Fred DeLuca discovered that marketing and visibility were key factors in the success of their two sandwich shops, named Pete's Super Submarines. When they opened their third location in 1967, they introduced the shorter, more memorable Subway name and its highly visible bright yellow logo.

Subway
SMART COMBO MEAL

- ◆ 1 12-inch Roast Beef Sandwich on whole wheat bread with mustard, lettuce, tomatoes, pickles, green peppers, and olives (no cheese, please, and hold the mayo!)

- ◆ 16 oz. diet soft drink

Nutrients	Target Values for one meal*	Approx. Values for this meal
Calories	666–833	622
Total Fat	22–27 gm.	10 gm.
Saturated Fat	7–8 gm.	6 gm.
% Calories From Fat	30%	14%
Dietary Fiber	8–10 gm.	13 gm.
Sodium	<800 mg.	1,990 mg.

Dietary Exchanges for this meal:

Carbohydrate	Vegetable	Meat	Fat
6	1	3 very lean	1/2

*Based on 2,000 to 2,500 calories per day

Good**for**You!

Satisfy your sweet tooth by ordering a smaller sandwich, a diet soft drink, and a cookie. Nobody says you can't enjoy a favorite food when you're watching your weight. Instead, cut back on the amount of food you eat and how often. You'll enjoy a cookie even more when it's a treat again and not a habit or a routine snack.

Trivia

Subway Sandwiches and Salads began franchising in 1974, nearly nine years after the original store opened. By 1997, there were over 13,000 Subway stores worldwide. Subway offers a relatively low-investment, low-overhead franchising program that five times earned it the top franchise opportunity by *Entrepreneur* magazine.

Subway
SMART COMBO MEAL

- **1 Deli Style Turkey Breast Sandwich with onions, lettuce, tomatoes, pickles, green peppers, and olives (hold the mayo!)**
- **1 Chocolate Chip or Chunk Cookie**
- **16 oz. diet soft drink**

Nutrients	Target Values for one meal*	Approx. Values for this meal
Calories	666–833	445
Total Fat	22–27 gm.	14 gm.
Saturated Fat	7–8 gm.	5 gm.
% Calories From Fat	30%	28%
Dietary Fiber	8–10 gm.	3 gm.
Sodium	<800 mg.	1,125 mg.

Dietary Exchanges for this meal:

Carbohydrate	Vegetable	Meat	Fat
4 1/2	0	1 very lean	2

*Based on 2,000 to 2,500 calories per day

Good **for** You!

Enjoy the crispy, crunchy taste of potato chips without the greasy fingers when you buy a small package of chips with the word "baked" on the label. While you're at it, look at the number of servings on the bag and see if you've been eating 1, 2, or even 3 servings when you eat the whole thing. Look for the number of servings in snack bags so you won't innocently overeat calories and fat.

Trivia

No grills and no deep-fat fryers make Subway the only major fast food chain where cooking is not done on-site. However, breads and rolls are baked at each store from dough that is prepared and shipped from a central location.

Subway
SMART COMBO MEAL

- **1 6-inch Hot Meatball Sandwich (if desired, add lettuce, tomatoes, onions, pickles, and green peppers without adding calories or fat)**
- **1 package baked low-fat Potato Crisps (1 1/8 oz.)**
- **16 oz. diet soft drink**

Nutrients	Target Values for one meal*	Approx. Values for this meal
Calories	666–833	550
Total Fat	22–27 gm.	18 gm.
Saturated Fat	7–8 gm.	6 gm.
% Calories From Fat	30%	30%
Dietary Fiber	8–10 gm.	5 gm.
Sodium	<800 mg.	1,260 mg.

Dietary Exchanges for this meal:

Carbohydrate	Vegetable	Meat	Fat
5	0	1 medium fat	1 1/2

*Based on 2,000 to 2,500 calories per day

QuickService✚theRightPrice =HighVolume & Profits

Fast food concepts like McDonald's, Burger King, KFC, and Pizza Hut build on these basics: a limited menu, standardized operations, and an established image. Chain restaurants streamline their menus, food preparation, and order taking to generate a high volume of business.

To keep food and labor costs low, fast food restaurants are self-serve instead of having table service, use disposable dishes and no dishwashers, and portion food precisely. Building design and kitchen layout maximize efficiency for quantity food production and rapid customer turnover. Take-out pizza places like Domino's and Little Caesar's also eliminate the expense of seating space.

Successful restaurant owners often invest their profits from their first location into a second and third restaurant. As the United States becomes saturated with fast food locations, chain operators open new locations in other countries as a way to continue their growth. Fast food chains are exporting this American way of eating.

Domino's
FAST FACTS

Ranked #9 in sales

Parent company: Domino's Pizza, Inc.

Headquarters: Ann Arbor, MI

Year founded: 1960 in Ypsilanti, MI

Founders: Brothers Tom and Jim Monaghan

Worldwide sales: $3,200,000,000

Number of stores worldwide: 5,950

One patent: Food delivery hot bag with electric hot plate

One memorable ad campaign/jingle: "A half hour or a half dollar off" (first delivery guarantee in 1973)

Charitable giving: Domino's Pizza Partners Foundation assists employees in times of special need or tragedy.

Good **for** You!

Pizza is meant for sharing, and that can help filling your hunger for companionship. Stick to this lower-calorie pizza order, and ask your buddies for the support you need to lose or maintain a healthy weight. You may be pleasantly surprised that they want your help and encouragement to lose weight, too!

Trivia

Early on, founder Tom Monaghan worked with suppliers to incorporate items that have become standard in the pizza industry: a sturdy corrugated pizza box with airholes to keep steaming pizza from getting soggy, and an airtight fiberglass container that keeps pizza dough soft and pliant prior to baking.

Domino's
SMART COMBO MEAL

- **3 slices of a medium Hand-Tossed Pizza with onion, green peppers, and fresh mushrooms**
- **12 oz. regular soft drink**

Nutrients	Target Values for one meal*	Approx. Values for this meal
Calories	666–833	670
Total Fat	22–27 gm.	16 gm.
Saturated Fat	7–8 gm.	8 gm.
% Calories From Fat	30%	22%
Dietary Fiber	8–10 gm.	7 gm.
Sodium	<800 mg.	1,100 mg.

Dietary Exchanges for this meal:

Carbohydrate	Vegetable	Meat	Fat
7 1/2	0	1 high fat	1/2

*Based on 2,000 to 2,500 calories per day

Good **for** You!

Order breadsticks instead of cheesy bread from Domino's and you'll be filling up on bread without filling out on fat. Dipping breadsticks in low-fat pizza sauce is a tasty and healthy alternative to adding fat from butter or margarine.

Trivia

The 30-minute delivery guarantee initiated by Domino's was made possible by the K.I.S.S. Principle: Keep It Simple, Stupid! Order taking and pizza preparation were streamlined in the early years by offering only two pizza sizes, just eight toppings, and one cola beverage.

Domino's
SMART COMBO MEAL

- **2 slices of a large Hand-Tossed Italian Sausage Pizza (with green pepper and onion)**
- **2 Breadsticks**
- **12 oz. regular soft drink**

Nutrients	Target Values for one meal*	Approx. Values for this meal
Calories	666–833	660
Total Fat	22–27 gm.	21 gm.
Saturated Fat	7–8 gm.	8 gm.
% Calories From Fat	30%	29%
Dietary Fiber	8–10 gm.	3 gm.
Sodium	<800 mg.	1,140 mg.

Dietary Exchanges for this meal:

Carbohydrate	Vegetable	Meat	Fat
7	0	1 high fat	1 1/2

*Based on 2,000 to 2,500 calories per day

Good**for**You!

No need to use a nutrition chart and a calculator at Domino's Pizza as long as you order a pizza with a hand-tossed crust and stick to the suggested number of slices and the lower-fat toppings. Which pizza toppings have the most fat? Watch out for sausage, pepperoni, bacon, hamburger, and extra cheese.

Trivia

In 1975, Domino Sugar sued Domino's Pizza for the right to use the name, so the next 30 new pizza stores opened by Domino's Pizza were called Pizza Dispatch—until the lawsuit was settled in 1980 in favor of Domino's Pizza.

Domino's
SMART COMBO MEAL

- **2 slices of a medium Hand-Tossed Pineapple and Ham Pizza**
- **1 Breadstick**
- **12 oz. regular soft drink**

Nutrients	Target Values for one meal*	Approx. Values for this meal
Calories	666–833	600
Total Fat	22–27 gm.	16 gm.
Saturated Fat	7–8 gm.	6 gm.
% Calories From Fat	30%	24%
Dietary Fiber	8–10 gm.	3 gm.
Sodium	<800 mg.	1,060 mg.

Dietary Exchanges for this meal:

Carbohydrate	Vegetable	Meat	Fat
6 1/2	0	1 medium fat	1 1/2

*Based on 2,000 to 2,500 calories per day

Good**for**You!

The downside of eating cheese pizza is that the cheese contains saturated fat, which may increase the cholesterol in your blood and lead to heart disease. The upside of eating cheese pizza is that the cheese is a concentrated source of calcium, which is essential for maintaining strong bones. Some people prefer eating cheese to drinking milk for calcium.

Trivia

To help ensure success in the pizza making and delivery business, franchises for Domino's Pizza are awarded only to people who have been managers of another Domino's for at least one year—in addition to meeting other financial requirements.

Domino's
SMART COMBO MEAL

- 4 slices of a medium Hand-Tossed Cheese Pizza
- 16 oz. diet soft drink

Nutrients	Target Values for one meal*	Approx. Values for this meal
Calories	666–833	695
Total Fat	22–27 gm.	21 gm.
Saturated Fat	7–8 gm.	10 gm.
% Calories From Fat	30%	28%
Dietary Fiber	8–10 gm.	6 gm.
Sodium	<800 mg.	1,500 mg.

Dietary Exchanges for this meal:

Carbohydrate	Vegetable	Meat	Fat
6 1/2	0	1 1/2 high fat	1

*Based on 2,000 to 2,500 calories per day

Location, **Location,** Location

They're everywhere—almost. Name a place with plenty of people, and quick-service restaurants will be there to supply your need for food.

Fast food locations started as free-standing buildings with plenty of parking (also called stand-alones) and counted on car traffic for their customers. Over time, locations with pedestrian traffic were developed, making fast food locations appear everywhere!

The income level of local residents also impacts the decision of where to locate a fast food restaurant. The lower the income of residents of a community, the less likely it is to have a major chain restaurant. And towns with higher-income residents are often successful in defeating requests to build fast food restaurants.

Here's where you'll find major fast food chains today: community malls, regional malls, strip malls, downtowns, kiosks, airports, outlet malls, discount stores, office complexes, stadiums, zoos, museums, military bases, hotel room service, travel plazas, grocery stores, hospitals, schools, and colleges.

Where can you avoid fast food? Prisons and places of worship.

Dairy Queen
FAST FACTS

Ranked #10 in sales; Ranked #1 in sales in Snacks and Sweets Restaurant Category

Parent company: International Dairy Queen, Inc., a wholly owned subsidiary of Berkshire Hathaway, Inc.

Headquarters: Minneapolis, MN

Year founded: 1940 in Joliet, IL

Founders: J. F. "Grandpa" McCullough and his son Alex

Worldwide sales: $2,540,000,000

Number of stores worldwide: 5,792

One old-time ad jingle: "Let's All Go to the Dairy Queen"

Charitable giving: Sponsor of the Children's Miracle Network Telethon, which benefits local hospitals for children

Good**for**You!

A simple switch to frozen yogurt for a cone, sundae, or a Breeze means you can enjoy a sweet treat without the saturated fat found in regular soft-serve. Frozen yogurt contains the same good nutrition of vitamins and minerals found in dairy products—but without the fat.

Trivia

Ice cream makers J. F. "Grandpa" McCullough and his son Alex knew already in 1927 that their customers preferred soft ice cream, but no retail equipment existed to dispense it. Eighteen years later they read about a patent for a softserve dispenser and contacted the inventor, Harry M. Otiz. They signed an agreement with him and opened the first Dairy Queen in Joliet, Illinois, in 1940.

Dairy Queen
SMART COMBO MEAL

- **1 Hamburger**
- **1 medium Yogurt Cone**
- **16 oz. diet soft drink**

Nutrients	Target Values for one meal*	Approx. Values for this meal
Calories	666–833	550
Total Fat	22–27 gm.	13 gm.
Saturated Fat	7–8 gm.	5.5 gm.
% Calories From Fat	30%	21%
Dietary Fiber	8–10 gm.	2 gm.
Sodium	<800 mg.	825 mg.

Dietary Exchanges for this meal:

Carbohydrate	Vegetable	Meat	Fat
5 1/2	0	2 medium fat	0

*Based on 2,000 to 2,500 calories per day

Good**for**You!

Combining a grilled chicken sandwich with a DQ sandwich means you'll eat fewer calories and fat than a standard combo meal with french fries. You can feel full without the fat!

Trivia

> During World War II, new softserve freezers could not be built because the materials were diverted for wartime. The McCulloughs continued to sell the rights to use the freezer in specified territories to potential store owners. The agreements were quite informal and did not include ongoing royalty fees because the McCulloughs thought the popularity of soft ice cream would be short-lived.

Dairy Queen
SMART COMBO MEAL

- **1 Grilled Chicken Sandwich**
- **12 oz. regular soft drink**
- **1 DQ Sandwich**

Nutrients	Target Values for one meal*	Approx. Values for this meal
Calories	666–833	610
Total Fat	22–27 gm.	15 gm.
Saturated Fat	7–8 gm.	4.5 gm.
% Calories From Fat	30%	22%
Dietary Fiber	8–10 gm.	3 gm.
Sodium	<800 mg.	1,190 mg.

Dietary Exchanges for this meal:

Carbohydrate	Vegetable	Meat	Fat
6	0	2 1/2 lean	1

*Based on 2,000 to 2,500 calories per day

Good**for**You!

It's tough to stop at a Dairy Queen and not order a DQ treat. If you must, dare to be different and skip the meat sandwich. Instead, combine onion rings with a yogurt treat to reduce both your calories and your saturated fat for this visit. To add just 50 to 80 calories more—and still stay under 700 calories total—add a Fudge Bar, a Starkiss, or a Vanilla Orange Bar.

Trivia

By 1950, there were 1,400 DQ stores selling cones, sundaes, pints, and quarts to take home. Milk shakes and malts were added in 1949, banana splits in 1951, and hamburgers, hot dogs, french fries, and onion rings in 1958. The Peanut Buster Parfait and Brownie Fudge Delight became popular novelties in the '60s. The introduction of Blizzards in 1985 swept Dairy Queen to the top as the #1 treat shop.

Dairy Queen
SMART COMBO MEAL

- **1 order of Onion Rings**
- **1 small Strawberry Breeze**

Nutrients	Target Values for one meal*	Approx. Values for this meal
Calories	666–833	640
Total Fat	22–27 gm.	16.5 gm.
Saturated Fat	7–8 gm.	4.5 gm.
% Calories From Fat	30%	23%
Dietary Fiber	8–10 gm.	4 gm.
Sodium	<800 mg.	405 mg.

Dietary Exchanges for this meal:

Carbohydrate	Vegetable	Meat	Fat
7	0	0	3

*Based on 2,000 to 2,500 calories per day

Good**for**You!

When you're hungry for a hot dog, order a DQ chili dog without the cheese. Combine it with a frozen yogurt sundae and diet soft drink to minimize the amount of saturated fat you eat. Saturated fat is the fat that can lead to heart disease.

Trivia

International Dairy Queen was bought in 1998 by billionaire investor Warren Buffett for $585 million. IDQ met his stock purchasing criteria: the business is well managed, it has a record of profitability, and it is a simple concept, not overburdened by technology.

Dairy Queen
SMART COMBO MEAL

- **1 Chili Dog (no cheese)**
- **1 medium Yogurt Strawberry Sundae**
- **12 oz. diet soft drink**

Nutrients	Target Values for one meal*	Approx. Values for this meal
Calories	666–833	580
Total Fat	22–27 gm.	18.5 gm.
Saturated Fat	7–8 gm.	7 gm.
% Calories From Fat	30%	29%
Dietary Fiber	8–10 gm.	3 gm.
Sodium	<800 mg.	1,100 mg.

Dietary Exchanges for this meal:

Carbohydrate	Vegetable	Meat	Fat
5 1/2	0	1 high fat	1 1/2

*Based on 2,000 to 2,500 calories per day

Pizza!**Pizza!**Pizza!

Pizza places rank second in popularity behind hamburger restaurants and account for 20 percent of all fast food sales. Two of the three leading pizza chains sell pizza only, offering delivery and pickup but no seating space for dining in.

Pizza wasn't always considered fast food. Authentic pizza crust is made with yeast, which gives the dough an airy, breadlike texture but takes time to rise. Pizza innovators perfected their recipes and systems to speed both the pizza preparation and delivery. Domino's guaranteed delivery within 30 minutes pushed every pizza restaurant to deliver faster.

Pizza has the potential to rank high in nutritional value when the pizza toppings are primarily tomato sauce, veggies like onion, peppers, and mushrooms, and small amounts of low-fat cheese such as mozzarella and parmesan. The popularity of pizza accounts for some of the increased consumption of cheese in the United States in recent years.

Little Caesar's

FAST FACTS

Ranked #3 in sales in pizza

Parent company: Little Caesar International, Inc.

Headquarters: Detroit, MI

Year founded: 1959

Founders: Michael and Marian Ilitch

Worldwide sales: $2,100,000,000

Number of stores worldwide: 4,300

One patent: carryout food tray

One memorable ad campaign: "Two pizzas for the price of one"

Charitable giving: Little Caesar's Love Kitchen Foundation operates two mobile restaurants that serve 100,000 needy people each year throughout the United States and Canada.

Good**for**You!

Make it easy to limit the number of slices you eat from a whole pizza. Share it with friends or family and remind yourself that controlling your weight means watching how much you eat and how often!

Trivia

Who can forget the television ads featuring outrageously long and rubbery "cheese pulls" that doubled Little Caesar's sales from 1988 to 1991. Humor in advertising has become a hallmark of Little Caesar's promotions.

Little Caesar's
SMART COMBO MEAL

- 2 slices of a medium Pan!Pan! Cheese pizza
- 1 Tossed Salad
- 1 packet fat-free Italian Salad Dressing
- 12 oz. regular Coke

Nutrients	Target Values for one meal*	Approx. Values for this meal
Calories	666–833	643
Total Fat	22–27 gm.	15 gm.
Saturated Fat	7–8 gm.	7 gm.
% Calories From Fat	30%	21%
Dietary Fiber	8–10 gm.	NA
Sodium	<800 mg.	1,400 mg.

Dietary Exchanges for this meal:

Carbohydrate	Vegetable	Meat	Fat
6 1/2	1	1 1/2 high fat	0

*Based on 2,000 to 2,500 calories per day

Good**for**You!

Add fruit or veggie finger foods for a refreshing addition to a pizza gathering. Choose grapes, strawberries, carrots, or apple slices for nibbling to keep from overeating pizza and pop.

Trivia

Pizza dough is made fresh daily at each Little Caesar's location, not at a centralized food preparation commissary. To ensure consistent quality, ingredients are supplied by Little Caesar's own distribution company, including Grade A cheeses, special flour, and all-natural spices.

Little Caesar's
SMART COMBO MEAL

- **2 slices of a medium Pan!Pan! Pepperoni pizza**
- **1 piece Crazy Bread**
- **12 oz. regular Coke**

Nutrients	Target Values for one meal*	Approx. Values for this meal
Calories	666–833	654
Total Fat	22–27 gm.	19 gm.
Saturated Fat	7–8 gm.	9 gm.
% Calories From Fat	30%	26%
Dietary Fiber	8–10 gm.	NA
Sodium	<800 mg.	1,070 mg.

Dietary Exchanges for this meal:

Carbohydrate	Vegetable	Meat	Fat
6 1/2	0	2 medium fat	1 1/2

*Based on 2,000 to 2,500 calories per day

Good**for**You!

Order extra sauce, not extra cheese, for a healthier pizza. Tomato sauce is a concentrated source of the antioxidant lycopene, which may reduce the risk of a heart attack.

Trivia

In 1992, K-mart and Little Caesar's began a joint venture that incorporated Pizza Stations and Pizza Express into 520 K-mart stores with food service operations. A thousand more K-marts will add Little Caesar's by 1999.

Little Caesar's
SMART COMBO MEAL

- **3 slices of a medium Pan!Pan! Cheese Pizza**
- **12 oz. regular Coke**

Nutrients	Target Values for one meal*	Approx. Values for this meal
Calories	666–833	693
Total Fat	22–27 gm.	18 gm.
Saturated Fat	7–8 gm.	9 gm.
% Calories From Fat	30%	23%
Dietary Fiber	8–10 gm.	NA
Sodium	<800 mg.	1,190 mg.

Dietary Exchanges for this meal:

Carbohydrate	Vegetable	Meat	Fat
7	0	2 high fat	0

*Based on 2,000 to 2,500 calories per day

Good **for** You!

Learn the locations where you can order pizza by the slice over your lunch hour. Satisfy your appetite for pizza, plus get away from your desk or out of your car or truck. A 10 or 15 minute break is the real thing, the pause that refreshes.

Trivia

Cofounder Michael Ilitch played professional baseball with the Detroit Tigers, but his career was cut short by a leg injury in 1955. After years of hard work as restaurateurs, the Ilitches became sole owners of the Detroit Tigers in 1992.

Little Caesar's
SMART COMBO MEAL

- 2 slices of a medium Pizza!Pizza! Cheese Pizza
- 2 pieces Crazy Bread
- 1 order Crazy Sauce
- 12 oz. diet soft drink

Nutrients	Target Values for one meal*	Approx. Values for this meal
Calories	666–833	688
Total Fat	22–27 gm.	20.5 gm.
Saturated Fat	7–8 gm.	10 gm.
% Calories From Fat	30%	27%
Dietary Fiber	8–10 gm.	NA
Sodium	<800 mg.	1,010 mg.

Dietary Exchanges for this meal:

Carbohydrate	Vegetable	Meat	Fat
6 1/2	0	2 high fat	0

*Based on 2,000 to 2,500 calories per day

TheFast Food Millionaire**Next Door**

Not everyone who owns or manages a restaurant has the makings to start the next big chain restaurant. The backgrounds of the founders of the top 12 chains give a clue about what it takes.

Fast food founders realized the value of hard work by the time they were teenagers and put in long hours at their restaurants. All paid attention to the details of their menu offerings, kitchen layouts, food preparation methods, food costs and menu prices, locations, and ways to attract customers. At some point, all recognized the value of advertising and promotion, particularly as more automobiles meant customers were more mobile—and hungry.

Most of these founders did not attend college, and a few didn't finish high school. All enlisted the support of their families as their restaurant's business and reputation grew.

As their fortunes grew, all made contributions to charitable causes in the communities that made their wealth possible. Some bought professional sports teams as a new challenge, including the San Diego Padres, the Detroit Red Wings, and the Detroit Tigers.

Fast food founders have changed the way America eats.

Arby's
FAST FACTS

Ranked #2 in sales in sandwiches

Parent company: Arby's Inc. (formerly a division of Triarc Companies, NY)

Headquarters: Ft. Lauderdale, FL

Year founded: 1964 in Boardman, OH

Founders: Brothers Forrest and Leroy Raffel

Worldwide sales: $2,060,000,000

Number of stores worldwide: 3,091

One memorable ad campaign: Arby's piles it on!

Good **for** You!

Roast beef sandwiches usually contain less fat than most hamburgers. But just like hamburgers, you can order them in different sizes, and that's where the added calories and fat begin. Stick to a regular size sandwich so you can wear your regular size clothes!

Trivia

Arby's got its name from the initials of its founders, the Raffel Brothers (R.B.), who started their first restaurant in Boardman, Ohio, selling roast beef sandwiches, potato chips, iced tea, and soft drinks.

Arby's
SMART COMBO MEAL

- **1 Roast Beef Deluxe Sandwich**
- **1 small order French Fries**
- **12 oz. regular Pepsi**

Nutrients	Target Values for one meal*	Approx. Values for this meal
Calories	666–833	695
Total Fat	22–27 gm.	23 gm.
Saturated Fat	7–8 gm.	6 gm.
% Calories From Fat	30%	30%
Dietary Fiber	8–10 gm.	6 gm.
Sodium	<800 mg.	1,075 mg.

Dietary Exchanges for this meal:

Carbohydrate	Vegetable	Meat	Fat
7	0	1 lean	3

*Based on 2,000 to 2,500 calories per day

Good **for** You!

Whatever happened to your New Year's resolution to lose weight? Consider getting on with your life as a person, not merely as someone who needs to lose weight. When you order smaller meals automatically, you can regain your identity and lift the weight from both your mind and your body.

Trivia

In 1991, Arby's was the first major fast food chain to introduce a complete line of lighter sandwiches and salads with less than 300 calories per serving. And in 1994 it became the first global chain to institute a no smoking policy in its company-owned restaurants.

Arby's
SMART COMBO MEAL

- **1 French Dip Sandwich**
- **16 oz. regular Pepsi**

Nutrients	Target Values for one meal*	Approx. Values for this meal
Calories	666–833	675
Total Fat	22–27 gm.	22 gm.
Saturated Fat	7–8 gm.	8 gm.
% Calories From Fat	30%	29%
Dietary Fiber	8–10 gm.	3 gm.
Sodium	<800 mg.	1,460 mg.

Dietary Exchanges for this meal:

Carbohydrate	Vegetable	Meat	Fat
6 1/2	0	3 lean	2

*Based on 2,000 to 2,500 calories per day

Good**for**You!

Think of five benefits to controlling your weight while you're eating this meal. Write those benefits down if it helps to remember them, then see if you can repeat them to yourself the next time you order fast food—or you can make up five more benefits every time you eat a lower-calorie meal.

Trivia

The Arby's chain was acquired by RC Cola in 1976, and 20 years later was spun off into a new public company, RC/Arby's, by its ultimate parent company, Triarc, a conglomerate of chemical and petroleum product companies based in New York.

Arby's
SMART COMBO MEAL

- **Chicken Fingers (2 pieces)**
- **Baked Potato (plain)**
- **1 oz. Arby's Sauce**
- **12 oz. diet Pepsi**

Nutrients	Target Values for one meal*	Approx. Values for this meal
Calories	666–833	675
Total Fat	22–27 gm.	17 gm.
Saturated Fat	7–8 gm.	2 gm.
% Calories From Fat	30%	22%
Dietary Fiber	8–10 gm.	7.5 gm.
Sodium	<800 mg.	965 mg.

Dietary Exchanges for this meal:

Carbohydrate	Vegetable	Meat	Fat
7 1/2	0	1 medium fat	1

*Based on 2,000 to 2,500 calories per day

Good**for**You!

Follow the 5-a-Day campaign to eat five servings of fruits and vegetables each day to reduce your risk of cancer. Try these simple ideas for one day: orange juice for breakfast, an apple or banana between meals, a tossed salad or coleslaw for lunch, a baked potato for dinner, and a small box of raisins to nibble while driving. That's an easy five in one day.

Trivia

Cofounder Forrest Raffel is a graduate of Cornell University's School of Hotel and Restaurant Administration, and brother Larry is a graduate of the Wharton School of Finance.

Arby's
SMART COMBO MEAL

- **1 Broccoli 'n Cheddar Baked Potato**
- **8 oz. regular Pepsi**

Nutrients	Target Values for one meal*	Approx. Values for this meal
Calories	666–833	670
Total Fat	22–27 gm.	20 gm.
Saturated Fat	7–8 gm.	5 gm.
% Calories From Fat	30%	27%
Dietary Fiber	8–10 gm.	9 gm.
Sodium	<800 mg.	600 mg.

Dietary Exchanges for this meal:

Carbohydrate	Vegetable	Meat	Fat
7 1/2	0	1/2 high fat	2 1/2

*Based on 2,000 to 2,500 calories per day

Hamburgers
Ranked by Calories, Fat, and Sodium

Chain	Weight	Calories	Fat	% Calories From Fat	Sodium
McDonald's	3.7 oz.	260	9 g.	31%	580 mg.
Hardee's	3.9 oz.	270	11 g.	37%	670 mg.
Dairy Queen	4.9 oz.	290	12 g.	37%	630 mg.
Burger King	4.4 oz.	330	15 g.	41%	530 mg.
Wendy's	4.7 oz.	360	16 g.	40%	580 mg.

French Fries
Ranked by Weight, Calories, Fat, and Sodium

Chain	Size	Weight	Calories	Fat	% Calories From Fat	Sodium
McDonald's	Small	2.4 oz.	210	10 g.	43%	135 mg.
Arby's Homestyle	Small	2.5 oz.	212	10 g.	41%	414 mg.
Hardee's	Small	3.4 oz.	240	10 g.	38%	100 mg.
Wendy's	Small	3.2 oz.	270	13 g.	44%	85 mg.
KFC		4.8 oz.	280	13 g.	42%	750 mg.
Arby's Curly Fries		3.5 oz.	300	15 g.	45%	853 mg.
Arby's Homestyle	Med.	4.0 oz.	340	15.5 g.	41%	665 mg.
Burger King*	Med.	3.6 oz.	340	17 g.	45%	680 mg.
Hardee's	Med.	5.0 oz.	350	15 g.	38%	150 mg.
Dairy Queen	Med.	4.0 oz.	350	18 g.	46%	630 mg.

*coated

Chain	Size	Weight	Calories	Fat	% Calories From Fat	Sodium
Burger King	Med.	4.1 oz.	370	20 g.	49%	240 mg.
Wendy's	Med.	4.6 oz.	390	19 g.	44%	120 mg.
Arby's Homestyle	Large	5.0 oz.	423	19 g.	41%	828 mg.
Hardee's	Large	6.1 oz.	430	18 g.	38%	190 mg.
Dairy Queen	Large	4.9 oz.	440	23 g.	46%	790 mg.
McDonald's	Large	5.2 oz.	450	22 g.	43%	290 mg.
Wendy's	Biggie	5.6 oz.	470	23 g.	44%	150 mg.
McDonald's	Super Size	6.2 oz.	540	26 g.	43%	350 mg.
Burger King*	King Size	6.0 oz.	590	30 g.	45%	1,110 mg.

Percent fat calculations may vary due to the rounding of numbers by the fast food company for calories and fat grams.

Shakes
Ranked by Size, Calories, and Fat

Chain	Item	Size	Calories	Fat	% Calories From Fat
Wendy's	Frosty	Small	330	8 g.	22%
Hardee's	Vanilla Shake		350	5 g.	13%
McDonald's	Vanilla Shake	Small	360	9 g.	23%
Arby's	Vanilla Shake	12 oz.	360	12 g.	30%
Burger King	Vanilla Shake	Med.	430	9 g.	19%
Wendy's	Frosty	Med.	440	11 g.	23%
Arby's	Choc. Shake	12 oz.	451	12 g.	24%
Wendy's	Frosty	Large	540	13 g.	23%
Dairy Queen	Choc. Shake	Small	560	15 g.	24%
Dairy Queen	Choc. Malt	Small	650	16 g.	22%
Dairy Queen	Choc. Shake	Med.	770	20 g.	23%

Soft Drinks vs. Milk
A Comparison of Nutrients

	Skim Milk 8 oz.	1% Milk 8 oz.	2% Milk 8 oz.	Whole Milk 8 oz.	Coke 12 oz.	Diet Coke 12 oz.
Calories	85	100	120	150	150	0
Carb.	12	12	12	12	38	.5
Protein	8	8	8	8	0	0
Fat	0	3	5	8	0	0
Sodium	125mg.	115mg.	120mg.	120mg.	15mg.	20mg.
Cholesterol	4mg.	10mg.	18mg.	33mg.	0mg.	0mg.
%DV Vit. C	4	4	4	4	0	0
%DV Vit. A.	15	10	13	7	0	0
%DV Calcium	30	30	30	30	0	0
%DV Riboflavin	20	20	24	23	0	0
%DV Iron	1	1	1	1	0	0

Worldwide Sales
1997

Chain	Worldwide Sales	Number of Stores	Average Yearly Sales per Store
McDonald's	$33,638,000,000	23,123	$1,454,176
Burger King	$9,800,000,000	9,400	$1,042,553
KFC	$8,200,000,000	10,237	$801,016
Pizza Hut	$7,300,000,000	14,400	$506,944
Wendy's	$5,226,000,000	5,207	$1,003,649
Taco Bell	$4,900,000,000	6,941	$705,950
Hardee's	$3,526,000,000	3,056	$1,153,796
Subway	$3,300,000,000	13,016	$253,534
Domino's	$3,200,000,000	5,950	$537,815
Dairy Queen	$2,540,000,000	5,792	$438,536
Little Caesar's	$2,100,000,000	4,300	$488,372
Arby's	$2,060,000,000	3,091	$666,451

Source: *Restaurants & Institutions*, July 15, 1998.

Franchise Fees

Chain	Franchising Started	Start-Up Costs	Min. Net Worth	Initial Fee	Royalty
McDonald's	1955	$407,600–646,350	$100,000	$45,000	12.5%+
Hardee's	1961	$699,000–1,740,000	$1,000,000	$15,000	4–5%
Burger King	1961	$73,000–511,000	$500,000	$40,000	3.5–6%
Wendy's	1971	$525,000–775,000	$750,000	$25,000	4%
KFC	1952	$722,000–1,122,000	$500,000	$25,000	4%
Arby's	1965	$525,000–850,000	$250,000	$25,000+	4%
Taco Bell	1964	$750,000	$1,000,000	$45,000	5.5%
Pizza Hut	1959	Information Not Available			
Domino's	1967	$150,000	N/A	N/A	5.5%
Dairy Queen	1944	$75,000–120,000	$15,000–30,000	N/A	4–5%
Little Caesar's	1962	$120,000–150,000	$20,000	N/A	5%
Subway	1974	$64,170–149,950	$275,000	$10,000	8%

Bibliography

1997 Directory of Chain Restaurant Operators, Chain Store Guide Information Services, Tampa, FL, 1997.

The 1998 Franchise Annual, Info Franchise News Inc., Lewiston, NY, 1998.

Ensminger, A. H., M. E. Ensminger, J. E. Konlande, and J.R.K. Robson; *Foods & Nutrition Encyclopedia,* 2nd edition, CRC Press, Inc., Boca Raton, FL, 1994.

Fast Food and Quick Service Restaurant Franchises: The North American Directory, Limulus, Yorktown Heights, NY, 1994.

Gerrior, S., and Bente, L. 1997. *Nutrient Content of the U.S. Food Supply, 1909–04.* U.S. Department of Agriculture, Center for Nutrition Policy and Promotion. Home Economics Research Report No. 53.

The International Directory of Company Histories. St. James Press, Chicago, IL, 1990.

Lundberg, Donald E., *The Hotel and Restaurant Business,* 6th edition, Van Nostrand Reinhold, 1994.

Restaurants and Institutions Magazine, July 1996.

Smith, Craig, *Giving by Industry: A Reference Guide to the New Corporate Philanthropy,* 1996–1997 edition, Capitol Publications, Alexandria, VA.

Trager, James, *The Food Chronology,* Henry Holt and Company, New York, NY, 1995.

Urdong, Laurence, and Janet Braunstein, *Every Bite a Delight and Other Slogans,* Visible Ink Press, Detroit, MI, 1992.

WEST BEND LIBRARY

613.28
R27

Reinhardt, Peggy.
Smart fast food meals

SEP 10 1999

DEMCO